Bob Chilcott

T0071045

5 songs for upper voices

MUSIC DEPARTMENT

OXFORD
UNIVERSITY PRESS

OXFORD
UNIVERSITY PRESS

Great Clarendon Street, Oxford OX2 6DP, England
198 Madison Avenue, New York, NY 10016, USA

Oxford University Press is a department of the University of Oxford.
It furthers the University's aim of excellence in research, scholarship,
and education by publishing worldwide

Oxford is a registered trade mark of Oxford University Press
in the UK and in certain other countries

© Oxford University Press 2007

Bob Chilcott has asserted his right under the Copyright, Designs
and Patents Act, 1988, to be identified as the Composer of these Works

Database right Oxford University Press (maker)

First published 2007

All rights reserved. No part of this publication may be reproduced,
stored in a retrieval system, or transmitted, in any form or by any means,
without the prior permission in writing of Oxford University Press,
or as expressly permitted by law. Enquiries concerning reproduction
outside the scope of the above should be sent to the Music Copyright
Department, Oxford University Press, at the address above

Permission to perform the works in this anthology in public
(except in the course of divine worship) should normally be obtained
from the Performing Right Society Ltd. (PRS), 29/33 Berners Street,
London W1T 3AB, or its affiliated Societies in each country throughout
the world, unless the owner or the occupier of the premises
being used holds a licence from the Society

Permission to make a recording must be obtained in advance
from the Mechanical-Copyright Protection Society Ltd. (MCPS),
Elgar House, 41 Streatham High Road, London SW16 1ER,
or its affiliated Societies in each country throughout the world

12

ISBN 978-0-19-335920-8

Music origination by Enigma Music Production Services, Amersham, Bucks.
Printed in Great Britain on acid-free paper by
Halstan & Co. Ltd., Amersham, Bucks.

Contents

All for Love of One 4

The Truth is Great 10

Circles of Motion 13

All things pass 20

Red Boots On 27

Composer's notes

All for Love of One: My intention with this piece was to write a real singing melody to reflect the passion and beauty of this fifteenth-century text. It is designed as a two-part piece, but can equally be performed in unison by singing the melody at bar 24 in the soprano part and at bars 31 and 55 in the alto part.

The Truth is Great: I wrote this piece for a festival in Denver, the theme of which was nature and the environment. The lyrics reflect on how small we are in the great scheme of things. To me the sentiment is not earnest but wistful, with a touch of gentle humour. This piece can also be performed as a unison song by omitting the alto part.

Circles of Motion: This poem, by the living native-American poet Joy Harjo, has a wonderful strength and an affirming message, again reflecting on the inevitable circle of life. I imagine this song being sung with verve and a sense of empowerment.

All things pass: I love the profound yet simple wisdom in this poem, which, as in the lyrics of the previous two songs, suggests that ultimately we have very little control over our destiny. I find this kind of sentiment very strengthening and comforting, so have written music that will hopefully inspire positive and empowered singing.

Red Boots On: This text was written by the English poet Kit Wright while he was living in Canada. I love this poem; it needs to be sung with a spikey, cheeky confidence, and have a touch of Joni Mitchell or the Chenille Sisters in the sound! The piece is written for four parts, but it can be sung with only two by omitting certain lines, as detailed in the footnote on the first page.

for the ABCD North West Honour Choir, Summer 2007

All for Love of One

Anon. 15th cent.

BOB CHILCOTT

If performing in unison, sing the soprano line in bars 24–31 and the alto line in bars 31–39 and 55–63.

© Oxford University Press 2007. Photocopying this copyright material is ILLEGAL.

13
a tempo
all, and all for love of one, and all for love of
16
one, and all, and all for love of one, for love of
20
one.
24
mf
S.
Thus am I ban - ished from my bliss By craft and false pre -
mf
A.
Thus am I ban - ished from my bliss By
mf

27
- tence, Fault-less, with-out of - fence, As of re -
craft and false pre - tence, Fault-less, with-out of-fence,
30
poco rit.
a tempo
- turn no cer - tain is. And all, and
no cer - tain is. And all, and all for
poco rit.
a tempo
33
all for love of one, and all for
love of one, and all for love of one, and

36
f
love, and all for love of one.
f
all, and all for love of one, for love of one.
f
40
S./A.
unis.
The run-ning streams shall be my drink, A-corns shall be my
43
food. No-thing may do me good But when of your
46
dim.
beau - ty I do think. And all, and all for
poco rit.
a tempo
p dolce
dim.
p dolce

49
love of one, and all for love of one, and
52
all, and all for love of one, for love of
55
S.
one.
mp espress.
And all, and all for love of
A.
one.
mp espress.
And all, and all for love of one, and
mp espress.

58
mf
one, and all for love, and
mf
all for love of one, and all, and all for
mf
61
p
all for love of one,
p
love of one, for love of one,
p
64
rit.
pp
unis.
S./A.
for love of one.
pp

Commissioned by The Young Voices of Colorado for the 2008
Sing a Mile High Children's Choir Festival, Artistic Director Jena Dickey

The Truth is Great

Coventry Patmore (1823–96) BOB CHILCOTT

If performing in unison, omit the alto line when the parts divide.

© Oxford University Press 2007. Photocopying this copyright material is ILLEGAL.

10
poco cresc.
3
Un - der high cliffs, and far from the huge town, I
poco cresc.
13
poco rit.
a tempo
S.
mp
A.
sit me down.
For want of me the world's course
mp
16
will not fail:
When all its
19
mf
espress.
work is done, the lie shall rot;
The

22
truth is great, the truth is great, and shall pre - vail,
mf espress.
25
f
poco rit.
the truth is great, the truth is great, and
f
28
a tempo
mf
unis. mp dolce
poco rit.
shall pre-vail,
When none cares whe-ther it pre-vail or not.
mf
mp dolce
32
a bit slower
p
rit.
The truth is great.
p

Commissioned by The Young Voices of Colorado for the 2008
Sing a Mile High Children's Choir Festival, Artistic Director Jena Dickey

Circles of Motion

Joy Harjo (b. 1951) BOB CHILCOTT

Music: © Oxford University Press 2007; Words: 'Eagle Poem' from *In Mad Love and War* © 1990 by Joy Harjo, reprinted with permission by Wesleyan University Press. Photocopying this copyright material is ILLEGAL.

15
S.
A.
more That you can't see, can't hear, Can't
18
mf
know ex - cept in mo - ments and in
mf
21
mp
S.
Cir - cles of mo - tion, cir - cles of mo - tion.
A.
mp
mp
25
p
f con forza
Like ea - gle that Sun - day morn - ing
p
f con forza
p
f con forza

29
S./A.
Cir - cled in blue sky, swept our hearts clean With sa - cred
33
wings.
37
S.
mp
A.
We see you, see our - selves and
mp sonore
41
S.
p dolce
know That we must take the ut - most care And
A.
p dolce
p dolce

45
mp legato
kind - ness in all things.
Breathe
mp legato
49
in,
breathe in,
mp legato
53
know - ing we are made of All this,
and

57
breathe, breathe in,
61
mf cantabile
know-ing We are tru - ly blessed be -
65
- cause we Were born, be - cause we Were born, be -
mf cantabile
be - cause we Were born, be - cause we Were
mf cantabile

69
- cause_ we Were born with-in a
born, be - cause_ we Were born with-in a
73
mp
cir - cle_ of mo - tion,_ cir - cle_ of
mp
mp
76
mo - tion.
p
80
S./A.
unis. p
Like_

84
ea - gle round-ing out the morn - ing, We
88
S.
A.
pray it will be done
poco rit.
8vb
92
unis.
a tempo
dolce
In beau - ty, in beau - ty,
dolce
96
rit.
slow
in beau - ty, in beau - ty.

Commissioned by the Ames Children's Choirs, Founder and Conductor Sylvia Munsen, for the Midwest Children's Choir Festival, Bob Chilcott, Guest Conductor 27 April 2007

All things pass

Lau-Tzu (6th-cent. BC)

BOB CHILCOTT

© Oxford University Press 2007. Photocopying this copyright material is ILLEGAL.

10
mp
All things pass.
mp
poco rubato
13
S.
mf espress.
All things, all things pass.
A.
mf espress.
All things pass, A sun - rise does not last all morn - ing.
mf espress.
15
All things pass.
f
All things
All things pass, A cloud-burst does not last all day.
f
All things pass,
f

18
pass.
dim.
All things pass.
poco più mosso
Nor a sun - set all night.
dim.
All things pass.
poco più mosso
mp
Ped.
21
S.
A.
mp
What al - ways chan - ges?
(Ped.)
24
What al - ways chan - ges?
unis. mf
Earth,
mf legato
(Ped.)

27
sky, thun - der, moun - tain, wa - ter,
29
S.
A.
Earth,
31
sky, thun-der, moun - tain, wa - ter,
34
f
Wind, fire, lake.
unis. mp espress.
These
f

37
change,
And if these do not last,
mp legato espress.
40
and if these do not last,
42
Do man's vi - sions last?
44
Do man's il - lu - sions last?

46
S.
A.
p
Take things as they come, take things as they
Take things as they come,
48
poco rit.
come.
take things as they come.
poco rit.
50
Tempo I
poco rit.
S./A.
mp poco rubato

53 unis.
a tempo
mp espress.
All things pass, A sun - rise does not last all morn - ing.
espress.
55
mf
All things pass, A cloud-burst does not last all day. All things pass,
mf
58
mp
Nor a sun - set all night. All things pass.
mp
61
rit.
p
slower
All things pass.
p

For the 30th Anniversary of the St Louis Children's Choirs, Artistic Director Barbara Berner.
A gift from Carna Manthey for Adrienne Broyles' Level I Children's Choir

Red Boots On

Kit Wright (b. 1944)

BOB CHILCOTT

If performing in two parts, sing the first and second soprano lines in bars 19–22 and 37–44, and the second soprano and second alto lines in bar 48–51.

Music: © Oxford University Press 2007; Words: © Kit Wright, used by kind permission of the author. All rights reserved.
Photocopying this copyright material is ILLEGAL.

10
f
win-ter - time.
She's got Red boots on, she's got
f
13
Red boots on,
Kick-ing up the win-ter Till the win-ter's gone.
16
Red boots on, she's got Red boots on, she's got Red boots on.
19
S.
Red boots on,
Oh Red boots on.
A.
mf

22
mf
Go by On-ta-ri-o, Look down Main, If you
mf
You can look down Main,
25
can't find Ma-ry Lou, Come back a-gain: Sweet light burn-ing In
You can come back a-gain:
28
f
win-ter's flame. She's got Snow in her eyes, got A
She's got
f

31
tin-gle in her toes And new red boots on Wher- ev- er she goes.
f
She's got Red boots on, she's got Red boots on,
34
Red boots on, she's got Red boots on, she's got Red boots on. Red boots on,
she's got Red boots on. Red boots on,
38
Oh Red boots on.

41
All a-round Lake Street, Up by St Paul, Quick-er than the white wind
44
Love takes all: Ma-ry Lou's walk-ing In the big snow fall.
47
S.
She's got Red boots on, she's got Red boots on,
A.1
She's got Red boots on, she's got Red boots on,
A.2
She's got She's got Red boots on,

50
Kick-ing up the win-ter Till the win-ter's gone. Red boots on, she's got
Kick-ing up the win-ter Till the win-ter's gone. Red boots on, she's got
she's got Red boots on,
53
S./A.1
Redboots on, she's got Red boots on. She's got Red boots on.
A.2
she's got Red boots on. She's got Red boots on.
1.
2.
55b
S./A.
She's got Red boots on. She's got Red boots on.
ff
S.
A.
ff